Introduction to Next Generation Compliance

Next Generation Compliance is an EPA initiative to increase compliance with environmental regulations by using advances in pollutant monitoring and information technology combined with a focus on designing more effective regulations and permits to reduce pollution. Protecting clean air and water, and ensuring our communities are safe from pollution, is more complex today than ever. Whether it's pollution that's not apparent to the naked eye or large numbers of small sources that collectively have a big impact on the environment, new challenges require us to innovate and improve. Today's challenges require a modern approach to compliance with new tools and approaches while strengthening vigorous enforcement as the backbone of environmental protection. Next Generation Compliance principles have been used to build compliance drivers into rules, permits, and enforcement settlements, resulting in better environmental performance, while also enabling regulators to more easily monitor and ensure compliance.[1] These principles are demonstrated by tools such as:

- public accountability through increased transparency of compliance data,
- electronic reporting,
- advanced pollutant monitoring for point source discharges,
- ambient monitoring in water bodies, both upstream and downstream from dischargers, and
- third-party verification of compliance with environmental requirements.

As authorized by the Clean Water Act (CWA), the National Pollutant Discharge Elimination System (NPDES) program controls water pollution by regulating point sources that discharge pollutants into waters of the United States. While Next Generation Compliance can and has been used across all environmental programs, this Compendium focuses primarily on use of Next Generation Compliance tools in the NPDES program to advance the goals of the CWA for point source discharges. These creative and innovative approaches illustrate how technological and behavioral advancements and efficiencies could improve compliance rates, increase transparency, and improve environmental performance. For more information about Next Generation Compliance in general, see http://www2.epa.gov/compliance/next-generation-compliance.

While some Next Generation Compliance tools have been implemented with existing resources, others will require regulators to address overall management of existing data systems, current capabilities, and long-term resource needs. The Agency expects that the E-Enterprise for the Environment Initiative (see http://www2.epa.gov/e-enterprise) will allow states, EPA, and tribes to collaboratively streamline

---

[1] For a discussion of theoretical and empirical literature on the effectiveness of individual-facility monitoring and enforcement in promoting compliance through deterrence, see, e.g., *Monitoring, Enforcement, & Environmental Compliance: Understanding Specific & General Deterrence* (Oct. 2007) (State-of-Science White Paper prepared for EPA), *available at* http://www.epa.gov/Compliance/resources/reports/compliance/research/meec-whitepaper.pdf; and U.S. EPA, Office of Enforcement and Compliance Assurance, *Compliance Literature Search Results – Citations to Over Two Hundred Compliance-Related Books and Articles From 1999 to 2007* (April 2007), *available at* http://www.epa.gov/Compliance/resources/reports/compliance/research/lit-results-2007.pdf.

business processes and drive and share innovations across agencies and programs. These efforts will support and build the foundation for more widespread use of Next Generation Compliance tools.

EPA's Office of Water has also issued several documents which present concepts that support Next Generation Compliance. These include:

- *Promoting Water Technology Innovation for Clean and Sate Water, Water Technology Innovation Blueprint -- Version 2* (April 2014)[2] and associated *Progress Report,* which promotes and supports technology innovation to restore, protect, and ensure the sustainability of our water resources, focusing on 'market opportunities' where technology innovation could help solve water challenges.[3]
- *Municipal Separate Storm Sewer System Permits: Post-Construction Performance Standards & Water Quality-Based Requirements – A Compendium of Permitting Approaches* (June 2014)[4], which consists of permit examples which demonstrate clear, specific, and measurable permit requirements and, where feasible, numeric effluent limitations in NPDES permits for stormwater discharges.

Format and Use of Examples Included in this Compendium

The NPDES examples included in this Compendium are grouped into the following categories:

- Transparency;
- Electronic Reporting;
- Advanced Monitoring;
- Third-Party Monitoring; and
- Innovative Enforcement.

Each section provides an introduction to a Next Generation Compliance tool and explains how that tool has been used to help advance the goals of the NPDES program; it then describes considerations related to use of that Next Generation Compliance tool in NPDES rules, permits, and enforcement settlements; and lastly, each section lists examples from the NPDES program which illustrate use of that Next Generation Compliance tool. The attached Appendix provides excerpts of the relevant rule, permit, or settlement language, as well as links to the complete documents, for some of the examples. Throughout the document, there are also text boxes with examples of creative and innovative Next Generation Compliance approaches in practice today in other environmental programs.

---

[2] Available at http://www2.epa.gov/sites/production/files/2014-04/documents/clean_water_blueprint_final.pdf.
[3] For additional information about innovations related to the CWA, see, e.g., the following documents: U.S. EPA, Office of Water, *Establishing Total Maximum Daily Load (TMDL) Wasteload Allocations (WLAs) for Storm Water Sources and NPDES Permit Requirements Based on Those WLAs* (November 2014), *available at* http://water.epa.gov/polwaste/npdes/stormwater/upload/EPA_SW_TMDL_Memo.pdf; Association of Clean Water Administrators, *Examples of State Innovations: Clean Water Act Compliance, a White Paper* (April 2013), *available at* http://www.acwa-us.org/.
[4] Available at http://water.epa.gov/polwaste/npdes/stormwater/upload/sw_ms4_compendium.pdf.

Each example in this Compendium demonstrates one or more Next Generation Compliance tools that are already in use in various NPDES contexts. By itself, this Compendium does not require the use of Next Generation Compliance tools in the NPDES program. Regions, states, and tribes may use these tools as appropriate and practical.

Transparency in the NPDES Program

What are the Benefits of Transparency?

Transparency has long been used in the NPDES program to make the performance of regulators and regulated parties more visible to the public – for example, requiring regulated entities to post information on websites (e.g., permit requirements, Discharge Monitoring Reports (DMRs), stormwater management plans, annual reports, Best Management Practices (BMPs)). Making information public in this way can improve the accountability and performance of regulators by making their decisions more visible and accessible. It can also make regulators more efficient as they can better access information to use and share. Transparency also enhances incentives for compliance.[5] It serves to increase public awareness, enabling regulated entities and the public to identify concerns and potential violations that should be addressed better by regulators or through direct stakeholder action.[6]

As an example of the benefits of transparency across an entire program area, EPA's Combined Sewer Overflow (CSO) Control Policy, and Clean Water Act section 402(q) adopting the policy as law, requires Publicly Owned Treatment Works (POTWs) with CSOs to ensure that the public receives adequate notification of CSO occurrences and CSO impacts. See 59 Fed. Reg. 18688, 18691 (April 19, 1994). Public notification can inform the public of the location of CSO outfalls, the actual occurrences of CSOs, the possible health and environmental effects of CSOs, and the recreational or commercial activities curtailed as a result of CSOs. Combining this required public notification with modern technologies, such as web posting or online maps, represents Next Generation Compliance. Sources themselves may be required to provide public notification, and/or regulators such as states or EPA can also advance public access by posting information or sending email alerts to interested parties who sign up to receive them.

Transparency in Rules, Permits, and Settlements

Reported information is more transparent when it is presented in a relevant format and with context understandable to the public. For example:

---

[5] See, e.g., Laplante, B., Lanoie, P. & Foulon, J., *Incentives for Pollution Control - Regulation and Public Disclosure*, No. 2291, Policy Research Working Paper Series, The World Bank (2000), *available at* http://ideas.repec.org/p/wbk/wbrwps/2291.html.

[6] See, e.g., Fung, A. & O'Rourken, D., *Reinventing Environmental Regulation from the Grassroots Up: Explaining and Expanding the Success of the Toxics Release Inventory*, Env. Man., Vol. 25(2), pp. 115–127 (2000), *available at* http://nature.berkeley.edu/orourke/PDF/tri.pdf.

- Depending on the purpose of the data, a live data feed or a near real-time posting of data may be useful. If a live online data feed could be difficult to understand and interpret, both for regulators and the public, lead time can be provided before information is posted. Some examples below have specified that posting should be soon after sampling and reports are due; some specify a particular timeframe.
- Posted information is more accessible if it is as few clicks as possible from the regulated entity's home page.
- Web postings that use plain language terms to describe the information allow Internet search engines to easily find the information.

Where information has been available for download, data formats such as CSV files allow for easier data analysis than, for example, PDF files. When information is available for individual facilities as well as in "drillable" summary form, data analysis becomes reproducible with online tools.

Communication, outreach, and educational materials can be used to provide guidance on how to interpret displayed data in the appropriate context related to national standards and health benchmarks. If users of state or EPA websites are able to easily report errors to the appropriate EPA or state data stewards, this helps expose data errors and improve the sources of the data over time.

Transparency Examples

The following examples of NPDES rules, permits, and settlements are grouped to show the types of transparency provisions implemented, such as for regulated entities to post information online, through public signage, or transmission of information through email or other electronic notifications. There are also examples of EPA- or state-run websites designed to provide information about water quality to the public.

Requirements to Post Relevant Information to the Web

- <u>Logan International Airport NPDES permit</u> requires the Massachusetts Port Authority (Massport) to make results of water quality sampling at airport outfalls available on the MassPort website. The website has links to each month's DMRs, as well as quarterly summaries, going back to 2008. Available at http://www.massport.com/environment/environmental-reporting/water-quality/monitoring-results/. See Appendix for more details.

- <u>The Middle Rio Grande Watershed Based Municipal Separate Storm Sewer System (MS4) Permit</u> requires public accessibility of the Storm Water Management Program (SWMP) document and annual reports online via the Internet and during normal business hours at the MS4 operator's main office, a local library, posting on the Internet and/or

> ➤ Innovations from Other Environmental Programs:

> During the Deepwater Horizon oil spill in 2010, BP placed cameras 5,000 feet underwater and streamed the live feeds over the Internet, allowing the public and the government to see the pollution and progress to cap the leaking well.

other readily accessible location for public inspection and copying. The permit also encourages the MS4 operator to hold a public meeting on the Notice of Intent (NOI), SWMP, and annual reports upon a showing of significant public interest. See Appendix for more details.

- City of Seattle, Washington NPDES Permit requires the city to implement web-based public notification system to inform the citizens of when and where CSOs occur. The process must include (a) mechanism to alert persons of the occurrence of CSOs and (b) a system to determine the nature and duration of conditions that are potentially harmful for users of receiving waters due to CSOs. Seattle and King County, Washington maintain a real-time public notification website that has CSO overflow information updated with available data every 10 minutes for King County sites, and every 60 minutes for Seattle sites. The King County and City of Seattle CSO website is available at http://www.kingcounty.gov/environment/wastewater/CSOstatus/Overview.aspx. See Appendix for more details.

- The EPA Multi-Sector General Permit for Stormwater Discharges Associated with Industrial Activity (MSGP) would allow a permittee to meet the public availability requirements for the stormwater pollution prevention plan (SWPPP) by posting its SWPPP on the Internet. The permittee would have to provide a URL in its NOI where the SWPPP can be found, and maintain the current SWPPP at this URL. Any SWPPP modifications, records, and other reporting elements required for the previous year would have to be posted at the same URL as the main body of the SWPPP. Confidential Business Information or restricted information may be withheld from public access, but such withheld portions must be clearly identified. See Appendix for more details.

- Metropolitan St. Louis Sewer District (MSD) 2011 consent decree (CD) requires MSD to post the following information on its website:
  - o All written submissions to EPA must be posted and remain on the site for three years;
  - o The CD itself must be posted on MSD's website and intranet website and MSD must direct all current employees, new employees, and any contractor or consultant retained to perform work under the CD to read the consent decree;
  - o A fats, oil, and grease (FOG) education information page; and
  - o A building backup clean-up guide produced in multiple languages.

  The website postings are available at http://www.stlmsd.com/our-organization/organization-overview/consent-decree. See Appendix for more details.

Requirements to Post Information at the Discharge Point[7]

- City of Cambridge, Massachusetts & City of Chelsea, Massachusetts NPDES permits require the permittee to post signs at all CSO structures. The signs must be a minimum of 12 inches by 18 inches in size and should either include a symbol for CSOs or be in additional languages if

---

[7] Even though posting signage, as contrasted with electronic notification of pollution discharges, is a low-tech and static form of public notification, requirements for regulated entities to provide public notice at CSO or sanitary sewer overflow (SSO) outfalls in an easily understandable format is becoming a more widespread practice and is an easily-implementable way to provide notice to communities.

determined that the primary language of a substantial percentage of the residents in the vicinity of a given outfall structure is not English. The Cambridge permit also requires signs at public access locations, and other sites as identified by the Massachusetts Department of Environmental Protection. See Appendix for more details.

DC Water's Potomac River CSO indicator light.

- <u>As part of an EPA enforcement settlement, District of Columbia Water and Sewer Authority (DC Water)</u> must operate CSO Event Indicator Lights to notify river users of CSO discharges. The Potomac River light, pictured here, is located on the River's north shore, near the mouth of Rock Creek. Another light is located on the north shore of the Anacostia River in front of DC Water's Main Pumping Station. A red light must be illuminated during a CSO occurrence and a yellow light must be illuminated for 24 hours after a CSO has stopped. The CSO Event Indicator lights are operated via remote signals originating from nearby the CSO outfalls responsible for the event conditions. See Appendix for more details.

Metro St. Louis Sewer District SSO discharge sign.

- <u>EPA issued administrative compliance orders to Metropolitan St. Louis Sewer District</u> to require MSD to post 24 inch by 18 inch signs at all streams, creeks, drainage ditches, and swales receiving SSO discharges. The orders also require MSD to notify the public about the posting of these discharge signs through annual customer bill inserts as well as on the MSD website. These notices include a description of where each sign will be installed in relation to the constructed SSO; why the sign is being installed; and a phone number so anyone observing a discharge can call to report it. The notices are available at http://www.stlmsd.com/sites/default/files/education/448845.PDF. See Appendix for more details.

- <u>Jersey City Municipal Utilities Authority (JCMUA) consent decree</u> requires JCMUA to post and maintain signs within 10 feet of all CSOs. The signs must be visible to the unaided eye from land and water from a distance of 100 feet. The consent decree also requires an authorized representative of JCMUA to certify that all signs have been posted and remain in place. See Appendix for more details.

State Regulations that Require Posting of Signs at all Discharge Points

- <u>Ohio EPA's regulations</u> require all NPDES permittees to post signs at their outfalls, including, but not limited to, discharges of process wastewater, non-contact cooling water, sewage or discharges from remediation sites, and bypass or combined sewer overflow discharges. The signs must include, at a minimum, the name of the permittee, the permit number, and the outfall number printed in letters not less than two inches high. The sign must be a minimum of two feet by two feet and the bottom of the sign must be a minimum of three feet above the ground. See Appendix for more details.

- <u>New York regulations</u> require permittees who discharge to surface waters to post signs not less than 18 inches by 24 inches with the permit number, the name and telephone number of the permittee, and the name, address and telephone number of the State regional office in which the discharge is located. See Appendix for more details.

Email or Text Alerts of SSO and CSO Discharges

- <u>New York's Sewage Pollution Right-to-Know Act</u> requires the New York Department of Environmental Conservation (NYSDEC) to develop regulations to require POTWs and operators of publicly owned sewer systems (POSSs) to report untreated and partially treated sewage discharges to NYSDEC and New York State health department within two hours of discovery and to the public and adjoining municipalities within four hours of discovery. NYSDEC is working with the NYS Division of Homeland Security and Emergency Services to transition all POTWs and POSSs to use the NY-Alert mass notification system for reporting sewage releases and distributing this information to the public. A single online form through the NY-Alert system was made available in early 2015 and is being used to notify the appropriate parties for two-hour notification and the public for the four-hour notification. See Appendix for more details.

- <u>Metropolitan Water Reclamation District of Greater Chicago (MWRDGC) NPDES permits</u>[8] require MWRDGC to develop a public notification plan. Under this plan:
  - o The public can sign up for daily emails and/or text messages when a confirmed CSO event or diversion to Lake Michigan occurs.
  - o MWRDGC posts a map of the city's waterways, color-coded based on CSO data compiled by District staff. Blue segments indicate that no CSOs have been confirmed by the District. Red segments indicate a confirmed CSO occurrence in that segment or in a segment upstream.
  - o MWRDGC is required to install two-sided weatherproof signage at CSO outfall locations.

  More information about the public notification plan, including how to sign up for notifications, is available at http://www.mwrd.org/irj/portal/anonymous/overview. See Appendix for more details.

> ➤ Innovations from Other Environmental Programs:
>
> Under the Safe Drinking Water Act, information is provided to the public with appropriate context through the annual consumer confidence report for drinking water systems, providing customers with information on how well the community water system is treating their drinking water.

---

[8] Stickney Water Reclamation Plant NPDES Permit; Calumet Water Reclamation Plant NPDES Permit; North Side Water Reclamation Plant NPDES Permit; James C. Kirie Water Reclamation Plant NPDES Permit; and the Lemont Water Reclamation Plant NPDES Permit.

- <u>City of Cambridge, Massachusetts & City of Chelsea, Massachusetts NPDES permits</u> require the permittees notify local health agents and local watershed advocacy groups by email within 24 hours of the onset of CSO discharge events and issue an annual press release discussing past CSOs. Cambridge is also required to include the following information on its website:
  - General information regarding CSOs, including their potential health impacts;
  - Locations of CSO discharges in the Charles River and Alewife Brook watersheds;
  - The overall status of all CSO abatement programs;
  - Web links to CSO communities and watershed advocacy groups; and
  - The most recent information on all CSO activations and volumes in both watersheds.

  The website postings are available at http://www.cambridgema.gov/theworks/ourservices/stormwatermanagement/combinedsewer overflows1/combinedseweroverflowcsodata/2014csoevents.aspx and http://www.ci.chelsea.ma.us/Public_Documents/ChelseaMA_DPW/water%20&%20sewer%20se rvices. See Appendix for more details.

- <u>NYSDEC's Division of Water</u> allows the public to sign up for email notifications of water related topics through the Making Waves subscription service. Topics include a weekly SSO and known CSO discharge report summary, listing the number of Sewage Discharge Reports received and the total reported volume for that week. The weekly alerts also provide notification of harmful algae blooms, with links to maps and other relevant information. Sign-up for the email notification is available at https://public.govdelivery.com/accounts/NYSDEC/subscriber/new.

EPA-Hosted Websites Providing Information about NPDES Permit and Enforcement Data, as well as Related Water Quality Information

- <u>EPA's Enforcement Compliance History Online (ECHO) website</u> provides integrated compliance and enforcement information for about 800,000 regulated facilities nationwide. Its features range from simple to advanced, catering to users who want to conduct broad analyses as well as those who need to perform complex searches. Specifically, ECHO allows you to find and download information on: (1) permit data; (2) inspection dates and findings; (3) violations; (4) enforcement actions; and (5) penalties assessed. See http://echo.epa.gov.

- <u>EPA's DMR Pollutant Loading Tool website</u> helps the public determine who is discharging, what pollutants they are discharging and how much, and where they are discharging. The tool calculates pollutant loadings from permit and DMR data from EPA's Integrated Compliance Information System for the National Pollutant Discharge Elimination System (ICIS-NPDES). Data are available from the year 2007 to the present. Pollutant loadings are presented as pounds per year and as toxic-weighted pounds per year to account for variations in toxicity among pollutants. The tool ranks dischargers, industries, and watersheds based on pollutant mass and toxicity, and presents "top ten" lists to help the public determine which discharges are important, which facilities and industries are producing these discharges, and which watersheds are impacted. The tool also includes wastewater pollutant discharge data from EPA's Toxics Release Inventory (TRI). Users can search TRI data to find the facilities with the largest pollutant discharges to surface waters or sewage treatment plants. Users can also compare the DMR data search results against TRI data search results and vice versa. See http://cfpub.epa.gov/dmr/.

- <u>EPA and USGS's Water Quality Portal</u>: EPA and the United States Geological Survey (USGS) co-developed the Water Quality Portal to provide a single, user-friendly Web interface to water quality data collected by federal, state, and tribal agencies and other water partners. It combines physical, chemical, and biological water quality data from multiple data sources at one location and presents the data using a common nomenclature known as the Water Quality Exchange (WQX). Since its April 2012 launch, the Portal has received thousands of visitors and delivered millions of water quality records. In addition, a third source has been added to the Portal: the U.S. Department of Agriculture's Agricultural Research Service STEWARDS database, making 168 new sites and over one million new watershed research records available. The web platform also enables use on any phone, tablet, or desktop. See http://www.waterqualitydata.us/.

- <u>EPA's "How's My Waterway" application and website</u> helps people find information on the condition of local water bodies from their smart phone, tablet, or desktop computer. The program uses Global Positioning System (GPS) technology or a user-entered zip code or city name to identify nearby waterways as unpolluted, polluted, or unassessed. Once a specific lake, river, or stream is selected, the site provides information on the type of pollution reported for that waterway and what has been done by EPA and the states to reduce it, along with simple descriptions of each type of water pollutant, including pollutant type, likely sources, and potential health risks. A map-oriented version of "How's My Waterway" was specifically designed for museum kiosks, displays, and touch screens. See http://watersgeo.epa.gov/mywaterway/.

State Applications and Websites that Provide Searchable Information about NPDES Permits and Water Quality Issues

- <u>Connecticut's two-part Public Act: "An Act Concerning The Public's Right to Know of a Sewage Spill"</u> requires the Connecticut Department of Energy and Environmental Protection (DEEP) to 1) provide a map indicating the combined sewer overflows anticipated to occur during certain storm events, and 2) to post notice of unanticipated sewage spills and waters of the state that have chronic and persistent sewage contamination that represents a threat to public health. DEEP has met the first part of the Act with a website map that currently shows CSOs and is in the process of expanding this map to all bypasses. The State is also developing software to make the communications between municipalities and the website interactive, e.g., by having forms with checks to ensure completeness and providing for an automatic email to the State to review and follow up on any reported bypasses. DEEP's CSO map is available at http://www.ct.gov/deep/cwp/view.asp?a=2719&q=525758&deepNav_GID=1654. See Appendix for more details.

- New York posts Excel files to its website listing all daily reports of untreated and partially treated sewage overflows from POTWs and POSSs that reach surface water bodies, helping the public to avoid contact with these waterbodies. To address wet weather CSO discharges, NYSDEC hosts a CSO Wet Weather Advisory web page of all CSO outfall locations in New York, including information about the receiving waterbody and CSO events. Available at http://www.dec.ny.gov/maps/nyscsoslink.kmz (requires Google Earth to be installed on your computer to view).

- Vermont Department of Environmental Conservation (DEC)'s website allows the public to obtain a report of any sewage release that reaches waters of the State. Releases appear on the website within one working day of receipt by State staff. DEC is developing a web application which will allow POTW operators to electronically self-report sewage releases, which will then be viewable by the public in real time. DEC anticipates that automatic notifications to subscribers via e-mail message will also be available to the public. For the current sewage overflow inventory website, see https://anrweb.vt.gov/DEC/WWInventory/SewageOverflows.aspx.

- California's State Water Resources Control Board maps SSO overflows in the state of California. The website allows users to search based on: 1) volume of flow; 2) date, local agency, county, street address, specific regional water board office; or 3) all incidents or just those incidents with valid GPS coordinates. Note that the map does not include overflows from the treatment plant portion of the systems. See http://www.waterboards.ca.gov/water_issues/programs/sso/sso_map/sso_pub.shtml.

CalEPA's SSO map.

- Washington State Department of Ecology maintains a Water Quality Permitting and Reporting Information System (PARIS), which contains information on water quality permits, inspections, enforcement actions, and discharge monitoring data. Both NPDES and State Waste Discharge permits are included in the database. See http://www.ecy.wa.gov/programs/wq/permits/paris/paris.html.

- Alabama Department of Environmental Management (ADEM)'s eFile system allows the public and other stakeholders to freely access documents that exist in electronic format in ADEM's document management system. The system has over one million documents available for the public to search, including permits, inspection reports, complaints, compliance reports, and enforcement actions. See http://app.adem.alabama.gov/eFile/.

- Florida Department of Environmental Protection uses OCULUS, an electronic document management system, to allow for public access to records associated with the State's waste, water, and air programs, including Florida's NPDES program. Documents available for searching include administrative files, enforcement correspondence, permits, SWPPs, and sampling results. See http://depedms.dep.state.fl.us/Oculus/servlet/login.

- Alabama's eComplaint system allows members of the public to electronically submit and track complaints through this system (even anonymously). The system allows complainants to provide detailed information, such as uploaded pictures, and the system quickly routes the complaint to the appropriate media department for response. The public can also search complaints received by the ADEM and what actions have been taken. See http://app.adem.alabama.gov/complaints/submission.aspx.

Electronic Reporting in the NPDES Program

What are the Benefits of Electronic Reporting?

Electronic reporting is rapidly replacing paper reports and creating many new opportunities beyond simply streamlining the transfer of information. Electronic reporting reduces costs associated with paper reporting and provides regulators with more complete and timely data, allowing more effective prioritization of monitoring and enforcement actions, as illustrated by the Ohio e-reporting example below. Electronic reporting typically entails use of an electronic "smart" form or web tool that guides the regulated entity through the reporting process. Simply emailing reports is not true electronic reporting.

On July 30, 2013, EPA proposed the NPDES Electronic Reporting Rule to require NPDES permittees to report electronically rather than through paper-based reports. The proposed rule, once finalized, would make Electronic DMRs (eDMRs) standard for all NPDES permits that require DMRs. It takes advantage of advances in information technology, expands EPA efforts to provide meaningful data to the public, and supports the EPA-wide effort to move from paper to electronic reporting. States will realize a significant reduction in reporting burden and cost savings due to electronic reporting from facilities rather than having to enter paper reporting into data systems. The rule has not gone into effect as of the issuance of this document, but in the interim, regulators have required electronic reporting where it is appropriate. For more information on the proposed rule, see http://www2.epa.gov/compliance/proposed-npdes-electronic-reporting-rule.

Many states are using eDMR systems for some or all compliance reporting, and many have eNOI systems as well. In Ohio, for instance, an eDMR system was implemented in 2007. By 2011, 100% of Ohio's NPDES permit holders were reporting electronically. According to interviews and data collection conducted by Ohio EPA, electronic reporting of NPDES DMRs produced significant efficiency savings of both time and resources, in addition to increasing data quality. The application makes data submission and correction easier. The eDMR application automatically reviews submitted information and flags any data that does not fit within defined parameters of the field or specific ranges. This flagged data is automatically summarized and sent to the permit holder, who is then able to correct errors made during submission, and resubmit the DMR.

Electronic reporting has improved Ohio EPA's ability to monitor and enforce CWA compliance. The automated compliance checks reduced errors by 90% per month, leaving Ohio EPA with more accurate and robust data. Ohio EPA saw a decrease in sample frequency violations. Ohio has also received positive feedback from the regulated community. Simultaneously, as the need for data entry and error checking diminished, Ohio EPA was able to move almost five full-time personnel away from those tasks and into other types of work. Ohio EPA has expanded electronic reporting through its eBusiness Center to air pollution, drinking water, solid and hazardous waste, and water/wastewater operator exams.

Electronic Reporting in Rules, Permits, and Settlements

EPA issued a new policy statement on electronic reporting in September 2013 providing:

> "We are establishing a new Agency-wide policy on e-reporting that specifies in developing new regulations that we will start with the assumption that reporting will be electronic and not paper based. And we will used shared services to do this to the maximum extent possible. This Policy Statement is one important step forward in the Agency's larger E-Enterprise for the Environment Initiative."

While e-reporting reduces paper transaction costs associated with creating, mailing, entering, and error correction, it also necessitates new efforts to create the necessary tools to assist the regulated source in submitting quality reports and software to accept the electronic submittals.

Electronic Reporting Examples

The following examples show EPA and state tools for accepting electronic reporting submittals, as well as examples of permit requirements for NPDES regulated entities to report electronically.

Examples of EPA tools for Regulated Entities to Report Electronically

- NPDES Electronic Reporting Tool (NeT) is a tool suite developed by EPA to facilitate direct electronic submittal of data by the regulated community. It uses commercial "off-the-shelf" software and can support diverse form and data submission formats.

- NetDMR is a national tool for NPDES permittees to submit DMRs electronically via a secure Internet application to EPA through the National Environmental Information Exchange Network. NetDMR allows participants to discontinue mailing in hard copy forms to meet reporting requirements under 40 CFR 122.41 and 403.12. NetDMR was developed under an EPA grant by a consortium of states coordinated by the Environmental Council of States (ECOS), EPA, and led by Texas. NetDMR provides a generic, open standards-based, CROMERR-approved eDMR system. The application can be implemented by U.S. EPA, by a state, or by any other organization with the authority to accept DMRs. See https://netdmr.epa.gov/netdmr/public/home.htm.

> ➤ Innovations from Other Environmental Programs:
>
> The Greenhouse Gas Reporting Program is a Clean Air Act program that requires over 8,000 facilities across 40 industry types to monitor GHG data, including emissions, and report them to EPA on an annual basis. Facilities use an electronic system to calculate and submit their data to EPA, which runs real-time checks for common mistakes. If a potential mistake is detected, EPA sends the reporter an electronic message prompting corrections within a 45-day verification period. The electronic system also runs thousands of post-submission verification checks on the reports to flag potential errors for EPA staff to further investigate as appropriate. In 2014, EPA began publicly flagging facilities with unresolved errors or ones that did not provide a valid reason for an absent report, and their facility pages contained cautionary text about the errors. This improved data transparency and accountability.

Examples of State Tools for Regulated Entities to Report Electronically

- Alabama's Electronic Environmental (E2) DMR Reporting System Program: ADEM is providing a Web-enabled electronic environmental (E2) reporting system for wastewater facilities to streamline the management of DMRs and SSO reports required under Alabama's wastewater regulation program. The E2 DMR and SSO system provide wastewater facilities with an alternative way to submit DMR and SSO data and allow ADEM to electronically validate the data, acknowledge receipt, and upload data to the state's central wastewater database. ADEM offers this electronic reporting to its regulated facilities and participation is required in most formal enforcement actions and in all NPDES permits as they are issued or re-issued. See https://e2.adem.alabama.gov/NPDES.

- Wisconsin's DNR Switchboard is a secure e-business portal which allows individuals to apply for wastewater permits online and electronically report monitoring forms, including DMRs, for facilities regulated under the Wisconsin Pollutant Discharge Elimination System program. See http://dnr.wi.gov/topic/Switchboard/.

- Ohio eDMRs (see description above, under "What are the Benefits of Electronic Reporting," and Appendix for more details). See http://www.epa.ohio.gov/dsw/edmr/eDMR.aspx.

Requirements for Regulated Entities to Report Electronically

- Vessel General Permit (VGP) requires vessel owners/operators to submit all NOIs, Notices of Termination (NOTs), annual reports, and DMRs electronically, unless EPA grants the owner/operator a report-specific waiver from electronic reporting. This limited waiver is available, for example, if the owner/operator has issues regarding computer access or they are located in an area that is underserved by broadband access. Information submitted electronically is publicly available and downloadable through an EPA-maintained online search tool for the permit. More information on the VGP and the electronic reporting system are available at www.epa.gov/npdes/vessels. See Appendix for more details.

- Multi-Sector General Permit (MSGP) requires most submittals under the permit to be submitted via EPA's NeT or NetDMR. Waivers based on limited computer availability or capability would only be granted on a one-submittal basis, i.e., the next submittal must be electronic unless the permittee applies for and receives an additional waiver. See Appendix for more details.

- General Permit for Offshore Subcategory of the Oil and Gas Extraction Point Source Category for the Western Portion of the Outer Continental Shelf of the Gulf of Mexico requires all DMRs to be submitted electronically through NetDMR and all NOIs to be filed electronically using NeT. See Appendix for more details.

- EPA Region 10 has issued several NPDES permits in Idaho (the Cities of Grace, New Meadows, and Payette) allowing the permittee to submit monitoring data and other reports in either hard copy or through NetDMR. The City of Payette permit only allows paper reporting for six months after the effective date of the permit. After six months, the permittee must submit monitoring data and other reports electronically through NetDMR. See Appendix for more details.

- City of Chelsea, Massachusetts NPDES permit allows the permittee to submit monitoring data and other reports in either hard copy or through NetDMR for the first year after issuance of the permit. After the first year, the permittee must submit electronically unless it can demonstrate a reasonable basis which would preclude it from doing so. See Appendix for more details.

Advanced Monitoring in the NPDES Program

What are the Benefits of Advanced Monitoring?

Advanced monitoring refers to a broad range of sampling and analytic equipment, systems, techniques, practices, and technologies for better detecting and measuring pollution. Advanced monitoring includes 1) monitors that can measure discharges from a particular source and 2) those that monitor pollutants in the ambient environment.

Advanced monitoring technology generally fits into one or more of these categories:

- Monitors pollutants on a real-time or near real-time basis, often without lengthy lag times for laboratory analysis;
- Less expensive, easier to use, or more mobile compared to technologies currently in widespread use;
- Can provide data of acceptable quality and/or in greater quantity that is more complete or easier to interpret for a specific purpose;
- Is an existing technology but used in a new way to provide better information on pollutants, pollution sources, or environmental conditions.

Advanced monitoring can provide communities and individuals with real-time information about pollution that affects them.[9] Advanced monitoring technologies have also been used by regulators and communities to better identify significant pollution and noncompliance problems.[10] For instance, up- and downstream monitoring have been used to increase environmental stewardship and accountability, and could one day reduce the risk of violations and allow for quicker response to discharges or spills affecting water quality.

> ➤ Innovations from Other Environmental Programs:
>
> The Massachusetts Department of Environmental Protection (MassDEP) uses aerial photography to track areas of wetlands loss. MassDEP's Wetlands Loss Mapping Project has accurately located and mapped wetlands using an innovative GIS-based computer program and a wetlands mapping database. By comparing changes over time, these maps can identify wetlands that have been filled. This effort has developed reliable and verifiable data on location, acreage, and causes of wetlands loss beyond what permitting records reveal. MassDEP believes that a decline in acreage of wetland loss can be attributed in part to increased efforts to publicize the ability to capture wetland losses through aerial photography and in part to tough enforcement actions for confirmed substantive violations found through wetlands loss mapping.

---

[9] While there are differences between monitoring air and water pollution, some of the applications of advances in air pollution monitoring may be instructive for the NPDES program. See Snyder, Emily G., et al., *The Changing Paradigm of Air Pollution Monitoring*, 47 Env. Sci. & Tech. 20, 11369-77 (2013), *available at* http://pubs.acs.org/doi/pdf/10.1021/es4022602.

[10] See, e.g., O'Rourke, D. & Macey, G., *Community Environmental Policing: Assessing New Strategies of Public Participation in Environmental Regulation*, Association for Public Policy Analysis and Management, Vol. 22, No. 3, 383-414 (2003), *available at* http://nature.berkeley.edu/orourke/PDF/CEP-JPAM.pdf.

Due to differences in the reliability of sensor technologies, some monitors could be more useful for screening potential areas of concern rather than for compliance monitoring. Traditionally, the cost of installing and maintaining continuous monitoring sensors has been high when compared to traditional, intermittent sampling. However, as the technology drops in price, the scope of projects that are considered cost-efficient broadens. In addition, new tools are being developed by both governmental and private entities to communicate, analyze, and display the data gathered by these technologies.

EPA Region 6 is testing use of Continuous Surface Water Quality Monitoring Systems to promote pollution prevention, track compliance with settlements, and improve environmental conditions, particularly in remote areas. These systems consist of monitoring devices which include an automated wireless notification system which can send live data to a monitoring website, provide real-time status, and alert the company and regulator when a pre-set concentration threshold has been exceeded. In addition, EPA is involved with several efforts to promote innovative technology in various aspects of the water program:

- EPA's Office of Water (OW) and Office of Research and Development (ORD) worked with the Alliance for Coastal Technologies to sponsor a Nutrient Sensor Challenge to help accelerate the development and deployment of affordable nutrient sensors for water, including local watersheds, drinking water facilities, and wastewater systems. Sensors eligible for this competition will cost less than $5,000 to purchase, be deployable for three months without maintenance, and be ready for the commercial market by 2017. This effort is being hosted by the Challenging Nutrients Coalition, with the coordination of the White House Office of Science and Technology Policy. See http://www.act-us.info/nutrients-challenge/.
- EPA has supported the creation of 13 Water Technology Innovation Clusters across the country, who are leading the nation in water technology innovations through regional collaboration among businesses, government, research institutions, and others. See http://watercluster.org/wordpress/.
- On December 2, 2014, ORD also hosted an EPA Technology Innovation Showcase and Collaboration and Technology Transfer Seminar in Cincinnati, Ohio. The goals of the event were to: 1) feature new water technology coming out of the water cluster research program and other EPA technologies; 2) continue to draw attention to the OW Technology Innovation Blueprint; and 3) educate potential collaborators and EPA staff about opportunities to collaborate and how to get started. For an agenda of the event, see http://www2.epa.gov/sites/production/files/2014-11/documents/innovateshowcase_agenda.pdf.

When used by regulated entities, advanced monitoring can more effectively prevent and reduce pollutant discharges, or—even better—identify pollutant discharges before they become violations, often while making operations more efficient. For certain industry sectors with remote unmanned sites, such as some oil and gas disposal and production sites, using instream monitoring can help reduce accidental discharges of brine or produced wastewaters from tanks, batteries, flow lines, vessels, and retention berms. Some monitors, like conductivity detectors, are relatively inexpensive and stable. These technologies provide an option for a company to work cooperatively with regulators to reduce environmental impacts to tributaries, creeks, rivers, and lakes before expensive environmental damage is done.

Advanced Monitoring in Rules, Permits, and Settlements

NPDES Regulations, at 40 CFR 122.48, require state and EPA permit writers to "specify required monitoring including the type, intervals, and frequency sufficient to yield data which are representative of the monitored activity, including, when appropriate, continuous monitoring." Currently, permit writers can employ continuous monitoring technologies for flow, temperature, and pH. For instance, since 2001, EPA Region 1 has issued a number of permits with continuous monitoring requirements for temperature where there are cooling water considerations, such as from an industrial facility or a nuclear power plant. Many of these permits also have continuous monitoring requirements for flow and pH. See Appendix for more details. Although continuous measurement technology exists for other parameters, such as total organic carbon, specific conductivity, residual chlorine, fluoride, and dissolved oxygen, these technologies are not currently approved for compliance monitoring purposes. As these technologies become approved by EPA for NPDES compliance monitoring, they can be incorporated into permits as appropriate.

The methods which NPDES and Industrial User permittees may use for compliance monitoring appear in 40 CFR Part 136.[11] Where required, continuous monitoring methods must meet the quality assurance and quality control specifications of 40 CFR Part 136. A list of approved CWA methods can be found on EPA's website at http://water.epa.gov/scitech/methods/cwa/methods_index.cfm and includes an approved method for continuous pH measurement of drinking, surface, and saline waters, domestic and industrial waste waters:

EXCERPTED FROM TABLE IB—LIST OF APPROVED INORGANIC TEST PROCEDURES

Parameter	Methodology	EPA	Standard methods	ASTM	USGS/AOAC/Other
28. Hydrogen ion (pH), pH units	Electrometric measurement		4500-H+ B-2000	D1293-99 (A or B)	973.41, I-1586-85.
	Automated electrode	150.2 (Dec. 1982)			See footnote, I-2587-85.

When advanced monitoring techniques have been used, a number of technical and practical challenges associated with this emerging area of technology remain:

- Are the sensors appropriate for their intended purpose with regards to accuracy, reliability, and overall quality?
- How should appropriate quality control operations and metrics be incorporated into compliance monitoring?
- Do the sensors require regular operation, maintenance, and/or calibration? For example, if a sensor is located at a remote or unmanned location, should there be a regular schedule of

---

[11] *Available at* http://www.ecfr.gov/cgi-bin/text-idx?SID=37cec60f72b6d3b0a50b86bfc4313c43&mc=true&node=se40.23.136_13&rgn=div8.

operation and maintenance to ensure all monitors are in working order and properly calibrated?

- How should data be integrated that originates from multiple sensors (which may have different quality levels) or from multiple parties (e.g., government versus citizen)?
- How will the public and regulators use data generated by the sensors in a way to protect human health?
- What will the reporting requirements or approaches be for data obtained through advanced monitoring techniques?

Advanced Monitoring Examples

The advanced monitoring examples below include such technologies as improved water quality sensor technology, remote sensing, and satellite imagery.

Examples of Advanced Monitoring Requirements in NPDES Permits and Orders

- EPA Region 10 has issued several NPDES permits in Idaho (the Cities of Grace, New Meadows, and Payette) requiring continuous flow and temperature monitoring for effluent and continuous temperature monitoring for surface water. See Appendix for more details.

- City of Seattle, Washington NPDES Permit requires the city to monitor all permitted outfalls with operating automatic flow monitoring equipment for discharge location, discharge duration, discharge volume, and weather-related information (precipitation and storm duration). See Appendix for more details.

- Logan International Airport stormwater permit requires Massport to monitor the outfalls that drain the runways and the perimeter roadway. During winter storm events, the permit requires Massport to sample the drainage from the runways and the perimeters for ethylene glycol, propylene glycol, biochemical oxygen demand, chemical oxygen demand, total ammonia nitrogen, and two toxic additives to deicing agents, nonylphenol and tolyltriazole. The permit also requires whole effluent toxicity testing, in order to help determine whether the discharge causes, has the reasonable potential to cause, or contributes to an excursion above a numeric or narrative criterion for whole effluent toxicity. In addition, Massport is required to perform real-time monitoring of the airport's outfalls during a deicing episode, for parameters including temperature, dissolved oxygen, and conductivity, to be representative of a storm event discharge from each outfall. See Appendix for more details.

- The Middle Rio Grande Watershed Based MS4 Permit requires continuous monitoring of dissolved oxygen and temperature in the North Diversion Channel Embayment and at one location in the Rio Grande downstream of the mouth of the North Diversion Channel to ensure actions required by the permit are not likely to jeopardize the continued existence of any currently listed as endangered or threatened species or adversely affect its critical habitat. See Appendix for more details.

- <u>City of Fort Smith, Arkansas consent decree</u> requires Fort Smith to take samples from its storm water outfalls during dry and wet weather and test them for a variety of pollutants, including but not limited to, "human indicators" (such as ibuprofen) to determine whether human sewage is entering into the storm water system and discharging through storm water outfalls. See Appendix for more details.

- <u>City of Harrisburg, Pennsylvania consent decree</u> requires Capital Region Water (CRW) to identify long-term CSO activation monitoring equipment that is suitable for CRW's system. The consent decree requires CRW to develop and conduct a pilot study to evaluate several flow activation technologies. CRW will use the results of this pilot study to determine which technology to implement to send an alert each time a monitored CSO outfall begins discharging. See Appendix for more details.

- <u>GSP Management consent decree</u> requires implementation of a system whereby the facility manager responsible for environmental compliance receives an electronic notification within 24 hours of an effluent limit violation. See Appendix for more details.

- <u>San Antonio Water System (SAWS) consent decree</u> requires SAWS to implement a Water Quality Program Plan to detect and quantify the extent of bacterial concentrations in select receiving waters within its service area. The Water Quality Program Plan will measure bacterial concentrations of Escherichia coli (E. coli) and the human Bacteroidales marker using a quantifiable polymerase chain reaction method at designated stormwater outfalls in order to trace exfiltration from the sanitary sewer system. See Appendix for more details.

Existing Technologies Used in New Way to Provide Better Information on Pollution and Environmental Conditions

- <u>Under a Region 6 NPDES construction stormwater general permit</u>, one permittee is submitting inspection reports documenting BMPs through photographs along with descriptions of the condition and maintenance performed. This allows the regulator to easily see the condition of the BMP throughout the history of the project.

- <u>The City of Baltimore's SSO Reporting Mobile Application</u> allows City staff to quickly enter data and pictures associated with an SSO event on an iPad or other mobile device. An electronic form is then populated with this data and emailed to a predefined distribution list. The ability to report SSOs in the field allows for improved accuracy and real-time record keeping.

- <u>The City of Baltimore's Pollution Source Tracking Mobile Application</u> allows City investigators to map discovered illicit discharges to storm drains and streams, and to store data collected using the iPad or other mobile device. The application also allows staff to view Geographical Information Systems (GIS) layers of the City and historical investigation data.

- <u>The City of Santa Barbara and the University of California, Santa Barbara used sewage sniffing dogs to test the correlation of canine responses with human-specific waste markers</u> and the use of canines for tracking upstream drain networks, routine watershed reconnaissance, and investigation of illegal dumping by recreational vehicle dwellers. The main advantages of the method are the low cost per sample, real-time results, and the large area that can be covered in one day. The highlight of the City's work was locating a force main leaking into a storm drain.

EPA, State, and Local Use of Advanced Monitoring for Environmental Assessment

- Tillamook River, Oregon water quality monitoring network: The Oregon Department of Agriculture, Oregon Department of Environmental Quality, Tillamook Estuaries Partnership, and Oregon State University are cooperating to develop a water quality monitoring network in the Tillamook River, Oregon. The network employs three bacteria monitoring techniques: microbial source tracking for source determination, traditional water column grab sample E. coli analysis for long term trends, and real-time continuous E. coli monitoring. Real-time E. coli concentrations are provided to a website on a 2-minute interval continuously, providing a large amount of previously unobtainable data that illuminates 24-hour, 7-day-a-week bacterial fluctuations in the watershed.

- Washington State Department of Ecology (ECY)'s Marine Monitoring Unit conducts a variety of marine observations, including monthly sampling at 37 core monitoring stations. ECY uses a floatplane to cost effectively cover its widely distributed station network and provides aerial photos of Puget Sound water conditions during flight time between stations to document oil sheens, strong algal blooms, and debris, island, and sediment transport near the surface. The aerial information is published two days after collection in a report called "Eyes Over Puget Sound," which combines long-term monitoring data, high-resolution photo observations, satellite images, en route ferry data between Seattle and Victoria, British Columbia, and measurements from moored instruments. This report encourages ECY to optimize resources, increase the timeliness and representativeness of information, and boost the overall relevancy of the program's monitor activity in Puget Sound. See http://www.ecy.wa.gov/programs/eap/mar_wat/surface.html.

- Washington State ECY has attached sensors to the Victoria Clipper IV, a private ferry that transits passengers between Seattle and Victoria, British Columbia. The sensors measure phytoplankton concentrations, turbidity, freshwater influence, salinity, and water temperatures during the ferry's twice-daily runs and help ECY and the University of Washington better understand algae blooms, plankton food web interactions, river plumes, and changes over time in Puget Sound. ECY also has sensors attached to the State's public ferries to gather data, another example of finding cost-efficiencies by using existing vessels and partnerships to gather environmental data. See http://www.apl.washington.edu/project/project.php?id=ferries_for_science.

- Washington State ECY Nitrogen Monitoring on Bertrand Creek in the Nooksack Watershed. ECY initiated a three-year project to measure the effectiveness of water quality cleanup and management activities in the Bertrand Creek watershed, a sub-watershed of the Nooksack River in Whatcom County, Washington. The project involves both discrete sampling and continuous monitoring for nitrate and other water quality parameters at upstream and downstream stations. The data will be used to determine the movement (flux), continuous annual loading (yield), and behavior (seasonal patterns) of nitrate concentrations in the creek. Currently, two of these stations are transmitting live data via satellite to ECY's webpage every three hours. See https://fortress.wa.gov/ecy/wrx/wrx/flows/station.asp?sta=01N100#block9 and https://fortress.wa.gov/ecy/wrx/wrx/flows/station.asp?sta=01N060#block11.

- <u>Cleveland Metroparks is studying the hydrology of the Rocky River headwater streams</u> affected by runoff by utilizing real-time flow and water quality sensors to attain precise, short-interval hydrograph and water quality data. The continuous monitoring network monitors water flow data at six primary headwater streams with similar geology, catchment size, fall, and channel width but of varying hydrologic intactness. The sites include two moderately degraded, two severely degraded, and two reference streams. In addition, four water quality and quantity monitoring stations are installed throughout wetlands in the 2,600 acre Rocky River Reservation, with three sites at inlet locations and one at the outlet. Two additional sites are located at wetland outflows in West Creek Preserve, a 500-acre natural park. Each of these sites is equipped with a flow meter and a multi-parameter sonde with temperature, pH, conductivity, dissolved oxygen, and turbidity probes. Sensors connect to a data logger with real-time cellular telemetry. By comparing the inlet and outlet data, the research team is able to quantify the wetlands' exact levels of water storage and effectiveness at reducing pollutants.

- KCWaterBug: EPA Region 7, with the University of Missouri Kansas City, developed a website and app where citizens could access information and data on the lakes and streams in their neighborhoods, from multiple agencies and groups, in one simple location. The app, called "KCWaterBug," accesses real-time water quality monitoring stations using in-stream probes and satellite telemetry. Data from the stations is transmitted once an hour via satellites to servers at the University, where estimated E. coli concentrations are calculated using turbidity measurements and regression equations for each monitoring location. An hourly average estimated E. coli concentration for twelve streams is calculated and each stream is assigned a color code based on an index tied to health protective levels. The app is free and is available at http://www.kcwaters.org/kcwaterbug.html.

- <u>Real-time monitoring for cyanobacteria in Region 1</u>: EPA's New England Regional Laboratory owns and maintains two buoys in Massachusetts, on the Charles River and on the Mystic River, which have solar-powered water quality sensors that take measurements every 15 minutes and upload the results to a secure password-protected web site. Parameters measured include: temperature, conductivity, pH, dissolved oxygen, turbidity, chlorophyll, and phycocyanin. Phycocyanin measurement is used to estimate the level of cyanobacteria, which results during harmful algae blooms.

- <u>California State Water Resources Control Board's "Creek Watch"</u> is an iPhone application developed by IBM that enables members of the public to help regulators monitor thousands of miles of creeks and streams in their local watershed. Participants use the Creek Watch app to take and upload pictures of their local waterway and report how much water and trash they see. IBM's research lab aggregates the data and shares it with regional water boards to help them track pollution and manage water resources. All data is shown on a map and table on a publicly accessible website. The app is available for download at https://itunes.apple.com/us/app/creek-watch/id398420434.

- <u>Smart Phone Tagging at the Jordan River in Salt Lake County, Utah</u>: To raise awareness and promote community engagement in a local watershed, the Jordan River Commission, Salt Lake County, and the Center for Documentary Expression and Art developed an innovative outreach program funded by EPA's Urban Waters Small Grants Program. This project offers a technology-based approach to interpretation and turns the Jordan River Parkway into a nature center without walls. With a smartphone, participants can use the web app to map the Jordan River trail and identify "interpretive stops" that provide photographs, stories, poetry, as well as educational information about native trees, water quality, community destinations, and Jordan River history. Moreover, people can alert officials about maintenance or water quality concerns by using the "Report an Issue" button on the website. See http://www.myjordanriver.org/.

Other Uses of Advanced Monitoring to Model Water Bodies

- <u>The Intelligent River®</u> is a Clemson University project with real-time watershed-scale monitoring which will directly enhance efforts to assess the water quality of watersheds, rivers, and streams. Battery-operated computers called "MoteStacks" are inserted into buoy systems anchored to the river floor. External sensors collect data on water temperature, flow rate, turbidity, oxygen levels, and the presence of pollutants. The MoteStacks process the data and transmit it to Clemson University's high performance computer system for display on the Intelligent River® website. For more information, see http://www.clemson.edu/public/ecology/program_irre.html.

- The Jefferson Project is a collaboration among Rensselaer Polytechnic Institute, IBM, and the Fund for Lake George which has deployed 40 sensing platforms monitoring 25 variables such as weather, water chemistry and quality, lake currents, and stream flows. The project uses a supercomputer to model the lake and create a monitoring and prediction system. Local groups can use the data to make informed decisions on the protection of Lake George in New York. See http://fundforlakegeorge.org/JeffersonProject.

- Hudson River Environmental Conditions Observing System (HRECOS) is a network of water quality and weather monitoring stations in the Hudson River Watershed. It is funded by EPA, the National Oceanic and Atmospheric Administration (NOAA), the Hudson River Foundation, and the Hudson River Estuary Program of the NYSDEC. Stations record water quality (e.g., acidity, dissolved oxygen, turbidity, temperature, and suspended sediment concentrations) every 15 minutes and transmit data to the HRECOS website, where users can download data and create graphs of near real-time water and weather conditions. See http://www.hrecos.org/.

Third-Party Verification

Properly structured third-party monitoring and verification in rules, permits, and settlements can enhance accountability, improve compliance, and produce better compliance data.[12] Third-party monitoring, when combined with public disclosure, informs the public of the regulated entity's compliance status and enables public responses to noncompliance. Effective third-party verification approaches are structured to ensure that auditors are competent and independent and that audit or inspection criteria are objective and fact-based.[13] For instance, as in the example below, in order to ensure the third party is truly independent, data can be submitted concurrently to the government and not shared in draft with the regulated entity or its counsel for review. This process can build in allowances for correcting sampling or lab errors, while still allowing the regulator to ensure that the facility is not inappropriately influencing the content of the third-party report.

Third-Party Verification Example

- Alpha Natural Resources consent decree: Alpha, one of the nation's largest coal companies, Alpha Appalachian Holdings (formerly Massey Energy), and 66 subsidiaries agreed to spend an estimated $200 million on installing and operating wastewater treatment systems and implement comprehensive, system-wide upgrades to reduce discharges of pollution from coal mines in Kentucky, Pennsylvania, Tennessee, Virginia, and West Virginia. The consent decree requires an independent third party Environmental Management System (EMS) consultant to review and evaluate Alpha's compliance with the terms of the consent decree and an

---

[12] See, e.g., Kunreuther, H., McNulty, P. & Kang, Y., *Improving Environmental Safety Through Third Party Inspection*, Wharton School - U. of Penn. (Oct. 2001).

[13] See Lesley K. McAllister, *Regulation by Third-Party Verification*, 53 B.C. L. REV. 1, 22-23 (2012); and Esther Duflo et al., *Truth-Telling By Third-Party Auditors And The Response of Polluting Firms: Experimental Evidence From India*, 128 Q. J. of Econ. 4 at 1499-1545 (2013).

independent third party EMS auditor to develop and concurrently submit an EMS Audit Report to the defendants, EPA, and relevant state regulators. Any third party hired to perform a consultation or audit cannot have a direct financial stake in the outcome of the audit(s), inspection(s), or evaluation(s) conducted under the terms of the consent decree. See Appendix for more details.

Innovative Enforcement

Innovative enforcement combines the lessons learned in implementing Next Generation Compliance with new capabilities in analyzing larger data sets to better identify serious violators, ensure the integrity of electronic reporting, and more effectively and efficiently track compliance with settlements while supporting new approaches to improve compliance.[14]

Innovative State Enforcement Program Examples

- Oregon Expedited Enforcement Orders: Oregon, through rulemaking, has created a process for expedited enforcement orders (EEOs). EEOs are a means of issuing a notice of violation, civil penalty, and compliance order in one two-page document that is expedited because the responsible party can choose to accept the offer to settle their case by signing the EEO and agreeing to pay a lesser penalty than if the notice had gone through the regular enforcement process. Signing and payment of the lower penalty creates a final order by law. Expedited enforcement through EEOs saves time an inspector would spend writing a referral for the Office of Compliance and Enforcement (OCE), the time of both OCE and the inspector in drafting and consulting on the Notice, and subsequent time typically spent on informal meetings, hearings, settlement negotiations, and other enforcement transaction activities.

- New York Law Enforcement Ticketing for SPDES Violations: In 2010, NYSDEC Division of Water partnered with its Division of Law Enforcement (DLE) and Office of the General Counsel to establish a system to increase the compliance rate of construction sites regulated under the State Pollution Discharge Elimination System (SPDES) general permit program. Under this Construction Stormwater Statewide Enforcement Initiative, DLE Environmental Conservation Officers conducted site visits and were authorized to enforce basic compliance matters with the State SPDES program by issuing tickets for violations. In past practice, NYSDEC would first issue a Notice of Violation to the regulated entity to encourage a voluntary return to compliance; if the entity did not return to compliance, then formal enforcement action was warranted. Providing "ticketing" authority was a new first step in this process for some violators. Overall, this initiative resulted in prompt compliance measures as DLE and Department of Water staff observed immediate corrective actions from tickets, on-site discussions, or through additional compliance monitoring activities (e.g., drive-by inspections, phone calls, and site visits).

---

[14] For a report exploring the use of compliance rate data to drive inspection and targeting decisions, *see* New Jersey Department of Environmental Protection, *Compliance & Enforcement Target and Measure Initiative Final Project Report* (Oct. 2006).

- <u>Vermont DEC's Environmental Enforcement Officers</u> have the authority to issue Notices of Alleged Violations and field tickets for violations of State environmental regulations. Once an Environmental Enforcement Officer initiates an enforcement action, violators may pay a "settlement" fine in lieu of an appeal.

Additional Resources

For additional information about Next Generation Compliance, see the following documents:
- Cynthia Giles, *Next Generation Compliance*, The Envtl. Forum, Sept.-Oct. 2013, at 22, *available at* http://www2.epa.gov/sites/production/files/2014-09/documents/giles-next-gen-article-forum-eli-sept-oct-2013.pdf.
- U.S. EPA, Office of Enforcement and Compliance Assurance, *Use of Next Generation Compliance Tools in Civil Enforcement Settlements* (January 2015), *available at* http://www2.epa.gov/sites/production/files/2015-01/documents/memo-nextgen-useinenfsettlements.pdf.

Forthcoming:
EPA is considering creating additional tools and resources to provide examples of how Next Generation Compliance tools have been included in the NPDES program and in other environmental programs, such as the Clean Air Act and the Resource Conservation and Recovery Act. If you have suggestions for how to do this, please contact Chrisna Baptista at 202-564-4272.